108 Discourses on Awakening

Mark Griffin

Hard Light Center of Awakening

108 Discourses on Awakening © 1989-2012 by Mark Griffin,
Hard Light Center of Awakening
ISBN 978-0-975902-00-4

For more information about the **Hard Light Center of Awakening** please visit *www.hardlight.org*. The web site provides a complete listing of Mark Griffin's other books and CDs, as well as links to audiobooks, podcasts and PDF books.

The Hard Light Center of Awakening is an organization founded and directed by Mark Griffin as a forum for the study of spirituality and meditation. Mark Griffin is a Meditation Master who is firmly established in the advanced Nirvikalpa Samadhi states — rare strands of consciousness that lead to remarkable perception and spiritual accomplishment.

First Edition: 2004

Second Edition: December, 2012

I would like to thank and acknowledge the following people without whose help and energy this book would not exist.

Editorial:
Daniel Hayes Uppendahl,
Pauline Arneberg,
Pat Cookinham,
Lydia Reineck,
and Lloyd Aspinwall

Transcription:
Brian Stephens,
Geoff Greenspahn,
Ananda Grimm,
Tim Maloney,
and Karen Stephens

Layout & Design:
Mindy Rosenblatt / podPublishing

With special thanks to:
Charles Lonsdale

Table of Contents

The Siddha Lineage

Mark Griffin is a Westerner who was born in the 1950's in the Pacific Northwest. His early adult years were spent in the aggressive pursuit of higher knowledge and purpose.

While a young man, Mark's studies in art and music brought him to the San Francisco Bay area. There in 1976 he met his Guru, Baba Muktananda. After years of full-time immersion in the study of meditation, Mark encountered a milestone of extreme spiritual significance – entrance into the advanced state of consciousness known as Nirvikalpa Samadhi. After Muktananda died, Mark continued to study with the great teachers of the Kagyu tradition, Kalu Rinpoche and Chogyam Trungpa, who supported the maturing and stabilizing of his abilities.

In 1989, after attracting several interested students, Mark began to teach meditation. He and his students relocated to Los Angeles and started the Hard Light Center of Awakening, an association dedicated to the art and science of awareness of the Self.

When Mark Griffin met Baba Muktananda he immediately realized that Baba was his Guru, his true teacher. Baba's Guru was the great saint of India, Bhagawan Nityananda of Ganeshpuri. It is with the blessings of these remarkable Siddhas that Mark carries on his inspiring teachings.

Foreword

As I sit trying to find words appropriate to open the introduction to this book, I look up from my small office into a hazy sky of mottled blues and infinite clouds and see a hawk spiraling slowly upwards.

It seems an auspicious metaphor for the travels I have been fortunate enough to undertake with Mark Griffin and his Hard Light Sangha. From literal journeys in places like the wooded foothills of Northern California to the teeming lanes and timeless temples of India to sojourns of a more esoteric nature in inner realms, Mark has proven a fearless, grinning guide. And a teacher who is always ready to provide wind under the wings of his sangha.

In these turbulent times of uncertainty and strife, there remains something ancient and reassuring — yet totally contemporary — about his presence. In 108 Discourses on Awakening, Mark, a quintessentially American guru and teacher, offers us guidelines to transcendence that are all the more memorable for their astute clarity and unvarnished approach to the human condition. Here is simplicity and thoughtful revelation intertwined in cohesive balance. Yet this in no way minimizes the vast source of knowledge Mark imparts here. Although his lineage and learning are directly connected to no less a personage than the revered Muktananda, Mark has an innate ability to make limitless, eternal truths seem self-evident in their forthright honesty.

Using everything from Bugs Bunny to computer analogies to explore and explain the metaphysics of awakening to our true selves, Mark speaks to the Western soul who may feel the lexicon of Eastern deities and disciplines too foreign and forbidding to broach. By deftly bringing these concepts onto familiar soil, he teaches us these dynamics are truly universal and open to every one of us.

Interestingly, for someone who could easily be mistaken for an outsized biker or bouncer, I remember Mark as having an easy way of moving through India, not an easy task for someone of his physical stature. The narrow lanes and chaotic alleys seemed to open for him just as he helped to remove obstacles there for our group. During a week-long meditation intensive in Varanasi I experienced with the sangha, Mark provided an incredibly palpable anchor as we navigated intense energies. As we sat for long hours in a centuries-old Brahmin's refuge of ochre stone burnished by countless sunrises, Mark would eloquently relate the subtle subtext of what we were experiencing during breaks from our meditations.

Sitting on a raised dais underneath garlands of fresh flowers that embroidered the walls and arches, Mark would intuitively initiate monologues that never ceased to provide insight.

These daily sessions were invariably accompanied by sounds drifting in from the banks of the Ganges, just steps below on Raja Ghat. The rhythmic pounding of the aundry dhobis as they beat clothes against the stones, the thrum of riverboat engines and the laughter and shouts of children became part of a sublime chorus of chaos that wove into our experience.

Though you won't have these ambient textures to accompany you during your exploration through this book, I expect your experience will be no less profound.

As for the actual contents of the book, I'll leave that journey to you. Mark is much more articulate than I could ever be about relating concepts such as shaktipat, the divine nature of breath and the alchemy a guru performs to help us transform into our realized Self.

But one important theme you will find throughout is this: our human form is a gift that allows us to awaken to eternal possibilities we never imagined. And Mark allows us to see our inherent divine nature and claim our universal inheritance, which is to merge with the ocean of love, or God, from which we all emanate.

In the West, where we constantly focus on the ego—what we've achieved, what we're going to do, what the other guy has—Mark reminds us the mind is not a source of light, but is merely a reflection of the eternal light of our true and immutable deepest self.

Well, the hawk is back, I gotta go…

Eric Hiss, Los Angeles, March 2004.

"These Discouses describe the dynamics of awakening – the inner unfoldment of a human being."

Mark Duffy

THE SPIRITUAL JOURNEY

SPIRITUAL LIFE

THE HUMAN FORM

RIGHT CONDUCT

STABILITY

DEPTH OF BEING

LOVE

PLACES OF POWER

THE WARRIOR

PURIFICATION

AWAKENING

1. THE HUMAN FORM

You should understand that the human form is rare in this universe. There are very few human beings, very few. The human form is as rare as a star at midday. It's very special because the laws of human form are a perfect reflection of the laws of Ishvara; there is no second thing. This gives us incredible potency.

When a person goes from complete ignorance, trapped upon the wheel of samsara, to liberation in a single lifetime, the process of the transformation of identity involved is mind boggling and enormous. Yet the rigor of human architecture also has this enormous flexibility that includes all qualities. In the process of awakening, the human form even encompasses the quality of gods, gaining their powers and capabilities. As the forms of realization, mastery and enlightenment occur, even gods and goddesses are surpassed by the enlightened human.

2. Right Conduct

Having won the rare human birth and acquired the even rarer opportunity to awaken, carefully consider the conduct of your life. Live in such a way that the negative aspects are diminished and the positive aspects are increased.

To do this, you learn to pay attention to what's important and ignore what's not important. For example, it's important to come to know and understand the Self. There should be an ever-increasing desire to know God. This desire to know the Self should be reflected in your moment-to-moment existence. You should practice meditation and give rise to the activities that accelerate your awakening and the awakening of others.

All the fulfillment and happiness you seek lies along this path. Only the truth has fulfilled a single human desire. As you come to understand that, your practice will become increasingly resolute and fruitful.

3. STABILITY

When a powerful transmission of light enters your system, it continues to roll through you over the course of time until it has touched every part of you. When the pressure of the light really hits, up come those dark spots you've been avoiding.

Then you must learn how to hold the pattern of your life in place. You will go through what the light wants you to go through. This happens in different ways with different people, but always leads to some degree of disorientation. You need to keep your life stable and simple. When you are involved with a teacher, the structure of your daily life should be stripped down to its essentials. In this way, you'll maintain your balance under the stresses and strains of the awakening process.

4. DEPTH OF BEING

Human beings are very complex and ruled by emotions. They have a tendency towards judgment—"Now I'm doing well. Now I'm doing poorly. Now I feel good. Now I feel bad." The one thing I'm always saying is that there is something greater underlying all of this judgment. We must constantly look for that next degree of depth, that next layer of subtlety within our being, to find a deeper and more profound basis of existence.

The idea behind meditation and spiritual study is to leave the surface and swim in the depths of your own being. In doing so, you want to avoid disorientation, maintaining just enough identity to be present as you undergo the countless transformations and transitions within. This is the daily bread of life, let alone spiritual life. Spiritual life just ups the ante by accelerating the process.

5. PLACES OF POWER

A place of power occurs where spiritual activity of an extremely high caliber has taken place over time. This can happen naturally in the creation of the world or through the repeated actions of awakened beings. These locations become holes in time where countless beings have punched through to the universal ocean of consciousness. That consciousness, once it touches the world, remains in place forever. A place of power, once established, becomes a gateway to countless dimensions and planes. These doorways remain, even after civilization has cycled a hundred times.

6. LOVE

In the spiritual game, love is your best friend. When I speak of love, I'm not talking about the sentiment of love nor the feeling of love. I'm talking about the deep ocean of love—the power present at the first moment of creation. Love is the power of infinite cohesion and infinite attraction that holds all qualities together and brings all qualities to their resolution. Never assume you understand love. It is a mystery whose depths you'll plumb forever. It is that energy that gives you the courage, strength and fire of inspiration to walk this path to the end.

Love's nature is ecstatic and powerful beyond description. It can be reached by anyone at any time. Love is a quality of creation that is thoroughly omnipotent, thoroughly omnipresent. There is no place where it is not. It affects all human beings and when it touches us, even in the slightest way, everything is all right.

Love is like a message of peace. It causes the mind to still itself and dissolve. In that stillness we hear the silence and the message that exists in silence. Love is the one thing that never fails to heal the turbulence of spiritual transformation.

7. THE WARRIOR

I will teach you to exist in this world as a silent and powerful spiritual warrior. You will become an iron-willed seeker of truth. I will teach you how to remain steady in the face of the constant fluctuations of the world, how to maintain your purpose, how to be awake and face every aspect of life without reaction, without fear. I will teach you how to run deep, how to live all the days of your life in this world, and on the last moment of the last day to step across with freedom, purpose, and clarity of spirit.

I will teach you how to sit silently, how to wait, how to learn to discern what is important in this life and not be distracted by what is not important, how to see what is not obvious. This is the liberation of the warrior who experiences joy beyond the experience of good fortune, and whose heart is not broken by misfortune.

8. PURIFICATION

Having won the grace of the Guru, having gained the transmission of shaktipat, the warrior is in a positive condition. However, you should not react to this blessing by patting yourself on the back over and over again, telling yourself how good you are, how bright you are, how talented you are to have gotten this far. More often than not, association with the Guru will bring all your imperfections and impurities to the surface for resolution. Thus we hear stories of those who tread the path facing great difficulties, meeting greater and greater challenges along the way. This is all part of the process of spiritual purification.

9. AWAKENING

Your kundalini will be awakened. You will be drawn into the mandala of grace. The arc of your incarnations will be altered. Your life will be drawn to serve dharma again and again and again. You will be tempered by those experiences, and one day you will awaken.

Each moment carries within it the silent yet inexorable presence of the awakening of consciousness. The struggle of this study will take place in the field of your life. The simple presence of awakening will enter the house of your being and turn on one light after another in every room of that house.

CHALLENGES

CONSTANT DIFFICULTIES

PERSISTENCE

CHOICES

NOT CHOOSING

OPPORTUNITY

10. CONSTANT DIFFICULTIES

When we prefer that which is easy and beautiful and fear the approach of challenging conditions, we miss the point of existence and end up in a condition of increasing neurosis. Perhaps as an act of will, we are capable of holding things in balance to a certain point. But on the scales of life, if any one quality accumulates too much to one side, what does it do? It becomes its opposite.

On the other hand, if you experience a constant flow of difficulties, know that the negative weight of your karma is unfolding itself in a manageable way. This is one of the signs of grace. What you should fear is the absence of difficulties. This means they are all accumulating in a great ball and will come down on you like an avalanche. There is no avoiding both sides of the scale.

11. Persistence

The primary measure of your character is the ability to do what you set out to do. If you carry a decision, however difficult, through to its completion, whatever else people may think of you, they will admire your character.

When you demonstrate a dodgy approach to life's challenges, when you abandon the field at the first sign of trouble, you will get nothing done because difficulty is a part of life.

One of the signs of being experienced in life is that whatever the world and your fate bring you, you face difficulties with aplomb and creativity. As a more experienced human being knows, it's not the goal but the journey that matters. The concepts of victory and defeat are but a shadow play.

12. CHOICES

After enough lifetimes, your breadth of experience becomes so wide that you have a superabundance of information and this information begins to act as a poison. There is so much input that you can't think straight. You reach a point where you can form a logical argument for anything; you can talk a topic up or down with equal skill.

When this time comes, it's extremely valuable to develop the ability to discern the important from the unimportant in an endless field of possibilities. In the end you will have to make a choice, and inherent in every choice is the commitment of your life force, your entire spirit.

13. Not Choosing

Refusing to make a decision, which is really a decision in itself, is the one choice that is absolutely certain to generate disaster. What is important is the process of making choices and your commitment to those decisions. It doesn't matter if the end result is success or failure. The point is to commit to a decision, bring it to a conclusion, and experience its fruit. This process forms the basis of wisdom.

14. OPPORTUNITY

Why are some people born to great fortune, to great wealth, while others are born into such base need? At the same time, those who are born with everything, given every opportunity, are often made weak by the very bounty of their existence. The most negative qualities can emerge from that personality.

On the other hand, we see that a person born into a condition of lesser opportunity, having to struggle for everything, begins to shine with the virtue of hard-won lessons. This idea of opposites is constant and everywhere.

THE PATH WITH HEART

TRUE PATH

SELECTION

WITHIN YOU AS YOU

ENDURANCE

BALANCE

POWER

15. TRUE PATH

The path with heart is not about feeling good or feeling bad. Many have been led to believe that a path with heart has less suffering on it. Nothing could be further from the truth. There's just as much suffering on a path with heart as with any other.

But the path with heart has the virtue of being the true path for you. When good fortune comes your way, you will be able to move swiftly enough to take advantage of it. When bad fortune appears, you will be strong enough to withstand it.

16. SELECTION

All paths lead to the Self. You must have the intelligence and knowledge to illuminate the path you select. So choose the path with heart, the path that matches your nature and reflects your qualities. That is the key to success. A person who is by nature a soldier will not be happy being a gardener. A person who is by nature a gardener will not be happy in another role.

Making this choice takes wisdom, but if you choose wisely, the path serves both your awakening and the fulfillment of happiness in this life. The path with heart has mukti, liberation, and bhukti, fulfillment and joy in this world. It's possible to have both.

17. WITHIN YOU AS YOU

The path exists within you as you. Everyone is always looking — looking here, looking there — trying to find it. It's so close that if it were a snake it would bite you. That's because you, yourself, are the path. You arise as the path.

This is difficult for Westerners to understand because they are so linear-minded. You cannot see the path because you are the path itself. It's like trying to see your own eyeball; it can't be done. You can see it in a mirror but that's only a reflection. What you see of the path—the drama of your life as it unfolds—has many layers.

18. ENDURANCE

A path with heart connects you to the internal flow of life and all your strength flows from within. Following this path, you won't have a sense that you need anything or that something is lacking. You'll maintain an anchor to your identity and feel like yourself no matter how demanding the process becomes. Your attention won't be diverted, and, as a result, you'll burn through all your karma very quickly with a minimum of suffering and effort.

19. BALANCE

The transmission of grace is like a blast to the internal structure of your being. It tends to be disorienting. If the spiritual seeker is unable to remain balanced and continue functioning as the grace pours in, this disorientation becomes an obstacle. Selecting a path with heart will give you the balance and endurance you need to hold true to your course and see it through to the end.

20. POWER

If you are connected to the path with heart, you are in your adamantine position. Your power will be present for you. Your fighting spirit will be there when you need to face adversity. If you divide your energy among several paths, you will be easily toppled because your balance is faulty.

Usually a single lifetime has one fate. If you can find a true path with heart, it will carry you over the course of your life, and you will be surprised at how it works out. There is a quality of magic in this life. If you are truly connected to your center, reality itself will bend and serve that cause.

DEATH

APPROACHING DEATH

CALLING ON THE GURU

HUNGRY GHOSTS

21. APPROACHING DEATH

The best thing in approaching death is to have meditated enough so that you've heard the footsteps of death coming. When death strikes, you will know what it is. Even as you're dying, you'll know you're dying, and you'll sit up and go into the best meditation you can. You'll start noticing that it's very easy to draw all of your consciousness into the sushumna because that's where it wants to go. So instead of becoming frightened, you'll say, "Oh, I'm just meditating and I've done this a thousand times in a thousand meditations. I'm just going along with it."

As death happens, a powerful drama takes place. You feel a subtle regret because you know that everything is happening for the last time. You're not going to be allowed to come back to this house ever again. You're not going to see your loved ones ever again, at least not in this form or this setting. Get used to the idea of transience so you don't linger over that last regret too long. Death is a very tricky moment, and you need the best attention you can muster.

22. Calling on the Guru

If you call on the Guru at the moment of death, the Guru will appear. If you're confused, he/she will inform you that you've died. The Guru will produce an illusion where you are transported into a condition of liberation and delivered from the wheel of samsara. Through the grace of the Guru and of the lineage, your consciousness will be wrapped up and delivered from the power of the wheel. It's like Virgil guiding Dante through the Netherworld, but it's very fast. Because death is definitely recognized as a tricky moment, the Guru will go for the best outcome as fast as possible, not taking any chances.

23. HUNGRY GHOSTS

Those persons having very strong desires that went unfulfilled in life may have enough power to resist the winds of the bardo. They refuse to enter the bardo and instead become hungry ghosts. They have enough power to stay in the world and walk around. They can see the objects of their desire, but they can't fulfill them because they don't have a body.

They'll haunt an area or follow people around, feeding on the energy of others. They try to use this mental energy to reproduce a reality, but it never works, and they feel excessively embittered. They're called "hungry ghosts" because they possess a wild, anxious hysteria since they haven't been able to fulfill a single desire for a long period of time. You don't want that to happen to you.

SADHANA

DESIRE

FRUIT OF DESIRE

KARMA

CAUSE AND EFFECT

DISCRIMINATION

24. FRUIT OF DESIRE

Every time you generate action based on desire, you create very powerful waves that agitate the mind. And what is the fruit of desire? Anyone who has explored the subject knows that the fruit of desire is more desire—followed by more agitation. It is a bowl that is never filled.

Usually, after you have incarnated enough times, you'll say, "Well, I've tried to fill that bowl for 'X' number of lifetimes. I've never done it. So now I'm going to stop filling it and see what happens."

25. Karma

Karma is action generated by desire, and desire arises from the individual ego—that aspect of mind that sees itself as separate from creation. When the mind uses the senses to reach out and touch creation, it tries to force creation into generating the fruit of its desire, namely, what we want in our lives.

Yet this behavior is the source of suffering. Desire-based activity is the absolute cause of transmigration from one lifetime to another, and unfortunately, karma doesn't play out fast enough in a single incarnation to keep up with it. It accumulates, and we only fulfill a small percentage of our desires within a lifetime.

26. CAUSE AND EFFECT

You are bound by your karma; it is the law of cause and effect. Every desire must be fulfilled, however incidental or misdirected it was when you produced it. When you pulsed with the energy of life at that quality of desire, you produced a seed of karma inside your mind-stream that follows you from lifetime to lifetime.

Karma builds up inside your system, and you're literally caught in a time loop where the entire thrust of a given lifetime is to redeem karmic coupons you generated centuries ago.

27. Discrimination

What do you do about desire? You live a righteous life, meaning you decrease desire inside the fabric of your life. You become very aware of what your prominent desires are and work on those first. Then you gradually come down to the subtler ones. Finally you come to a place where the dynamic of your life is a completely calm lake, and you can begin to see into it. That is called dispassion.

Dispassion and detachment are the brother and sister of discrimination. When you have the ability to separate out the reflexes of desire, then and only then can the subtle frequencies of discrimination, which are the qualities of higher intelligence, appear. The mind finally becomes clear and calm.

SADHANA: DESIRE

THE VIRTUES

PURE ACTIONS

THE POWER OF LOVE

GENEROSITY

HONESTY

PATIENCE

HUMILITY

GRATITUDE

28. PURE ACTIONS

Know without the slightest doubt that for every action there will be an effect in the form of karma. This being so, we try to choose the purest actions to create the highest quality karma even as we expiate the karma of the past in this life.

As we live out our past karma, we want to avoid generating new karma that will be a future obstruction. We learn to limit our actions to those of the highest selfless nature, cultivating the qualities of compassion, kindness, friendship, generosity, love, and patience.

29. The Power of Love

Love is the power of infinite attraction. The great poet-saints tell us that the universe comes into being from love. The magnetic force of love gives rise to the universe. The sun gives light out of love. The wind blows out of love. These words are poetic but they also recognize the genuine metaphysical power and magnetism that cause all movement in creation.

So raise love within yourself, and direct that love towards your indwelling enlightenment. Love, focused with attention on your life force, will bring a powerful surge of energy from the deepest Self because the Self itself responds to love.

30. GENEROSITY

Within ourselves, we have the capacity to express love and transmute negativity. When negativity is expressed towards us by others, generosity is the quality of love that is most effective. Generosity implies enrichment of our own condition and the spreading of that enrichment to others. Generosity is all about increase.

31. HONESTY

Honesty is the fundamental pathway to acquire and deepen all virtues. It is simple, direct and the most important quality you can have in spiritual life. Honesty provides true direction in the seemingly arbitrary selection of choices and possibilities that you will face over the course of your lifetime.

Without honesty, you will slip and slide everywhere. You will never find the touchstone of reality within yourself, and, without this, you will become fatigued and confused very quickly.

32. PATIENCE

Frequently to improve a situation, the quality you need in greatest abundance is patience. Most often, the truth is finally glimpsed through patience. If you are shooting from the hip, chances are you are going to miss your mark because you moved too fast. You didn't gain access to the whole circuit; you didn't get all the information needed. The truth is almost never on the surface. Wisdom and experience are the fruits of patience — patience of heart, patience of mind, and the ability to become quiet and listen.

33. Humility

Always seek to establish a presence of emptiness and humility. This is the whole idea of spiritual life; you listen intently to every situation. No presupposition, no judgment, no set of expectations about anything.

When you see a person wearing three thousand dollars worth of clothes, you don't make any judgment about that. You see another person, a homeless person pushing a cart down the street, and you don't make any judgment about that. Anybody can be anyone; all are God. If there's one thing for sure in this world, it's that nothing is as it seems on the surface, not one single thing.

34. GRATITUDE

The essence of humility is listening, and one of the oldest brothers of listening humbly is gratitude. The fundamental philosophy of the American Indian, the original occupiers of this ground, was one of humility and gratitude towards all life. They hunted only the food they needed and thanked the spirit of the animal for nourishment and warmth. Their social system had respect for life and gratitude for the opportunity of life.

The medicine dance, the dance of existence itself, carries with it a message that all experiences are to be met as gifts from God, even those that bring about our end. Famous chiefs, when faced with the certainty of death in battle, went out of existence with a full heart, not bitter, not sorrowful. Your life is defined by your actions and your mode of death. Facing great difficulty increases your power.

MEDITATION

OPENING

THE BELLOWS BREATH

RECOGNITION

SURRENDER

STOPPING THE MIND

SOFT SPOT

COMPASSION

35. OPENING

Use the first moments of meditation to relax your body, releasing it to gravity. Sit with your spine straight. Square your shoulders with your hips. Rest your head on your shoulders. Feel as if there's a single fiber that reaches from the base of the spine, up through the center of the chest, through the shoulders, through the center of the head, and up through the top of the head. The top of the head should seem to be suspended from a single filament of a spider web.

Let the mind sit in its natural condition. Let the natural connectedness of the breath, the life force, body, speech and mind, seat itself in your system. Here's the key to meditations of the ecstatic equilibrium. It's as if you're a vase or a water tank that's sitting beneath the ocean. All you need to do is open and the ocean will pour in. Awaken!

36. The Bellows Breath

As the basis for meditation, form a connection with the breath as it moves in and out of your body. Connect to the sounds and sensations of the breath. Breathe through the nose using a process called the "bellows breath."

In essence, you treat the body like a bellows that moves the air in and out. As you breathe in, expand the solar plexus to produce a vacuum that draws the air very deep inside your system. Physically expand the solar plexus. To exhale, squeeze the diaphragm pushing the breath out. Breathe in— expand the diaphragm and abdomen, drawing the breath in. Wait a beat. Then squeeze the diaphragm and abdomen, pushing the breath out. Pranayama, breath control, is one of the anchors of meditation.

37. Recognition

Do not generate meditation. Simply recognize the presence of Atman within, arising fully awakened, fully conscious as your awakened self. You will find the vibration of the awakened Atman streaming, pervading, and spontaneously flowing. There's nothing to do but recognize it as such.

38. Surrender

We can gain great occult powers, have vast yogic skills, and yet still have very little experience of God. We so often make the mistake of using spiritual practice to add to our greatness, to add to our own splendor at the level of the personal identity. Spiritual experiences become credentials, like résumés. This only adds to the difficulty of hearing the voice of the divine within.

The essence of meditation is seeking the deepest point within ourselves, that point where we surrender to the inner presence of the divine. We offer up what we have for the sake of love with no promise of return or benefit. This surrender is the only true doorway to knowledge of the Self.

39. STOPPING THE MIND

In meditation, the ideal is to bring the mind to an absolute stop, no motion, no thought, no mind. All motion of the mind is just a phantasmagoria, an illusion. It's not worth anything. It's just spin on top of spin on top of spin. It's motion for the sake of motion.

To still that substance is one of the prime purposes of meditation. The goal is to make the mind like a deep, deep lake—absolutely still and crystal clear. Though thousands of feet deep, you can see the bottom from the surface because it's so clear and still. The lake just keeps getting darker and darker blue. It is radiant blue universal consciousness. That's what meditation is about.

40. Soft Spot

No matter how much you meditate, no matter how much you practice, until you shift your identity from the walls of your fortress to the malleable soft spot at the center of being and meditate from that place, for all practical purposes nothing has changed. The problem is, if you hang onto your walls too long, you will miss your own life. You will miss your own awakening. You will not participate in your own process of unfoldment, except at the most surface level.

To meditate from that soft center is a condition of absolute receptivity, vulnerability, creativity, and power. It is also the metaphysical basis of your own fate, your own destiny.

41. COMPASSION

When all is said and done, compassion is your soft spot. No matter how hard your armor, this spot must remain sensitive. This is the point you need to access in meditation. Don't meditate from your throne at the center of your fort. Go to that malleable spot within yourself and begin to meditate from that place. This is the place where you can be reached. Here you can be touched by the world and all sentient beings. Here you can be touched by God.

THE BREATH

MOTION AND STILLNESS

LIFE FORCE

REALIZING THE BREATH

AMPLIFIED EFFECT

42. Motion and Stillness

By paying attention to the movement of consciousness in and out of the body that occurs with the movement of the physical breath, you can produce an organized pulse of breath and prana. In the space between the breaths—the point where you are no longer breathing in or out—there's an absolute stillness.

Notice how your mind piggybacks on the breath. As you breathe in, your mind will ride the breath deep within, and when the in-breath stops, the mind will stop deep inside. When you breathe out, the mind will again follow the movement of the breath. When you are no longer breathing out but not yet breathing in, the mind will become still and glide into meditation.

43. Life Force

If you are sensitive, you'll notice an energy, a vibration, deep inside the breath. This energy is called prana—the life force. Bring your attention to the descending and ascending breath and to the underlying throb of prana in both. Blending your attention with the breath expands your alignment with consciousness and increases your ability to track it.

The prana moves from its point of origin in ecstatic equilibrium down into mundane equilibrium and back again to ecstatic equilibrium, and the cycle continues over and over. In other words, the prana comes out of eternity into the wheel of time, animates your life force inside the wheel of time, and then again returns and terminates in eternity—continually cycling between time and eternity.

44. REALIZING THE BREATH

I'm sure the last thing I'll say in this world is that the breath is the seed to everything. Quite literally, if you realize the breath, you will realize the Self. It is so direct. There is not the slightest bit of obscuration here. I'm not speaking in tongues. It's a direct deal.

45. Amplified Effect

If you were to sit and do the breathing exercises without a Guru, you would get a certain effect. But with a Guru and the grace of shaktipat, the effects of that same effort are increased one hundred-thousand fold.

I've blessed the Guru a thousand times a day because I've met people who didn't have a Guru who worked so hard and made only a minute amount of progress. By the Guru's grace, my spiritual practices were accelerated and amplified. My progress then happened very quickly. The grace of the Guru sets the infinite creative energy of the universe into motion in your system.

SADHANA: BREATH

GOD

INFINITE OCEAN

LONGING

MYSTERY

NO DISTANCE

46. Infinite Ocean

God is an infinite ocean, mysterious and impossible to comprehend. Yoga is the preparation and process of searching for and swimming in that infinite ocean. The legendary spiritual masters are simply beings that have swum in that ocean so long they've become perfected, but there was a time when they were just like you.

47. LONGING

Your spiritual ripening corresponds to the degree of your hunger to know God. There is both the degree of longing and the degree of consciousness of that longing—how badly do you want it and what are you willing to pay for it? You must make a decision about what you're willing to surrender to this indescribable and unknown quality called God or the Self. Then God comes in the form of Awakening.

48. MYSTERY

God cannot be summoned or evoked, nor can She/ He be created or imagined. God is a supra-reality, reflected in the mirror of our perception as a condition called totality. Every quality of God is off the meter of our perception. It's like trying to see an elephant with your face one-quarter inch away.

The great masters have generated a message that never wavers, never changes. The message is that God is already here within us, as us. And that's the joke! This message has never wavered. The day must come when we truly hear it, address it, and act accordingly.

49. No Distance

The idea of oneness with God is very powerful. However, there's a subtle trick we play on ourselves as we do our sadhana. Viewing the spiritual journey as a distance that we travel can be a very serious mistake if we conclude from it that God is far away.

If this happens, even yoga and spirituality are captured by maya and become more food for conversation. We console ourselves that it is a higher grade of conversation because it's spiritual conversation. We say that we are on approach, that there is still a safe distance between God and us. There is not. The blazing courage of that quiet recognition is where the action is.

GOD

THE GURU

THE NATURE OF THE GURU

ETERNAL SPIRIT

THE ALCHEMIST

THE BRIDGE

FREEDOM

MERCY

UNCHANGING

50. ETERNAL SPIRIT

The Guru is not a particular person or place, although it can be. The Guru dwells both within and without. Its function is to bridge the gap between the seen and the unseen, between what is eternal and what is transitory. The Guru first appears outside of you and then appears within. It awakens you. It eliminates that which is not true.

The Guru is a mystery and a blessing. The Guru must be present for grace to occur; it is the substance of grace itself. It gives what is needed and takes away what is obscuring. It is an eternal spirit, stainless and self-supporting.

51. The Alchemist

The Guru is the grace-bestowing power of God, the means of awakening, and a profound mystery. This infinite and eternal spirit, constantly abiding, arises in countless formations, even transcending and capturing the force of cause and effect. It arises without as the cause of awakening and arises within as the action of awakening.

How it occurs is the seed-essence of mysticism. It is the transformation of lead into gold. Committing the substance of your being is the key to entering this profound process. Every atom, every particle of one's self is plunged into the crucible of spiritual training which transforms the spirit.

52. THE BRIDGE

The Guru is the bridge between the constantly changing wheel of past, present and future and the infinite singularity we call God or Self. The Guru is the means for the unfoldment of consciousness and triggering the release of the soul. It is constant and lies within, waiting.

When we seek the fulfillment of desire, we are actually yearning for God. The unwise soul seeks fulfillment on every corner, in every tavern, in every lover's eyes. The Guru is the single seed within, that, when merged with Self, fulfills all desire. The Guru is the wish-fulfilling tree.

53. Freedom

Grace, that undeserved favor of spiritual opportunity, tips the scales, turns the wheel, and extracts you from the machine-like gears of samsara. The Guru has been given the authority, the power, and the ability to wipe your slate clean in a single gesture, freeing your consciousness from the wheels of samsara that so intensely press upon your mind and heart. The Guru's grace gives you a chance to look beyond samsara—that limited expression of consciousness—into the ocean of eternity.

54. MERCY

The Guru is the incarnation of mercy. There is one single Guru that flows in infinite directions like a sun and arises in countless times, places and personalities. Wherever the presence of mercy is required, the Guru incarnates and generates relief at a super-rapid rate from the relentless law of karma.

This is the gift inherent in the transmission of grace. Oceans of karma from past actions are vaporized instantaneously. The grace travels through layer after layer of your being as if it were peeling an onion.

55. Unchanging

The Guru is a truth that is present at all times and in all places. The dynamics of time and space that generate maya are always in motion, while the mind, one thought leading to another, is the fuel of samsara. If you want to find the Guru, look for that which is not moving, that which is deep and still and unchanging. Look for what lies beneath this constantly spinning phantasmagoria that causes forgetfulness. It is this forgetfulness that gives the illusion that you are lost, that you are forsaken, that the Guru is far from you. However, the truth is that the Guru is as close as your own self.

MEETING THE GURU

GREAT FORTUNE

GRAVITY

THE CONVERSATION

56. GREAT FORTUNE

A Guru is a fully awakened being that has mastered the human form. To come into contact with a Guru is of such great fortune that it cannot be measured. To even hear of them, to hear their names, to think a thought towards them, is to invite a flow of energy towards you of oceanic proportions. To come into contact with them or align your life with them is to be bound up in an incredible sweep of profound dharma, love, and will.

57. Gravity

Often, the first appearance of grace is an indwelling sense of gravity. Your consciousness, your form, and your mind take on a heaviness as grace mixes with your being. I can only describe it as an effect of gravity. There's a sense of warmth or heat as you feel parts of yourself expanding, getting heavier, and beginning to mix together. Allow those points of gravity within you to reach out to each other and blend. This begins to create cohesion, a unity producing a new level of attention.

58. The Conversation

When you meet the Guru, the conversation just starts rolling between you. What are you willing to do? How far are you willing to take this? What is the nature of your heart? What are your interests?

This conversation is immediate and very direct. Although it seems to happen in words, it happens from within, flowing from the inner depths of the spirit to the surface. The meaning of what I say is not contained in the words that fly across the room, hit your ears, and trigger your mind. Instead, our dialog takes place at the deepest levels of being and is immediate. The words that happen afterwards are just pointers to the truth.

BLESSINGS OF THE GURU

RAREST OF JEWELS

SHAKTIPAT

STILLNESS

HOLY FIRE

ENLIGHTENMENT

TRANSMISSION

FIRST JOY

59. RAREST OF JEWELS

When a person has gained shaktipat, the totality of the equation of God, Guru and Self appears in one place, at one time. This is one of the rarest of jewels, hard won over thousands of incarnations. It comes about when a person has brought the dynamics of positive and negative influences in their life stream into equilibrium. When this occurs, the opportunity for freedom becomes available, and God manifests in the form of the Guru. The presence of the Guru is brought into existence by the necessity of the liberation of the individual soul.

60. SHAKTIPAT

The Guru uses a form of speech called shaktipat. Once you enter into a conversation with the Guru, the kundalini is awakened and you can't turn it off. It's a doorway you step through, and, as in a Bugs Bunny cartoon, the doorway disappears and you can't go back through it. Your life changes forever. The kundalini, being oceanic and eternal, will always talk to you. As you engage in this conversation of awakening, you want to have truth and the highest ideals in the chalice of your heart.

61. STILLNESS

The first gift of the Guru is the stilling of consciousness. All the false spin and agitation inside the mind is brought to a point of stillness and equipoise. That's where spiritual power truly lies. That's where the unification appears. We are all a part of the Great Ocean, and any idea of separation is just an illusion, a false dream.

62. HOLY FIRE

The Guru does not hold out. The Guru is an incredible fountain that you drink from as deeply as you wish, as often as you can. But you must realize you're drinking holy fire. To the extent that you can, drink from this fountain of grace, drink to the depth of your heart's fulfillment. You will find that the Guru's grace will be the fuel of transformation in your life, and its power can be used in many ways. The secret to employing the spiritual force of grace is clarity of intent. Do you want to know the truth? If that's your will, if that's your intent, then the grace will go to this place and operate with the greatest efficiency imaginable.

63. ENLIGHTENMENT

The transmission of grace from the Guru releases the vibration of enlightenment within the human form. Before this, the individual usually exhibited patterns of behavior that were entangled with the fulfillment of desire. With the transmission of grace, a metaphysical and chemical reaction takes place in the heart and mind of the seeker, and enlightenment gets thrown directly on-line.

64. TRANSMISSION

Here's how a transmission works. Power from the highest planes is brought into the sphere of practitioners through the grace and authority of the teacher. In this way, you, as a student, gain access to a level of light you wouldn't be able to enter on your own until you were much further down the line. By being able to access it now, you can make an enormous leap in a single instant. You go from where you are at that moment to a higher level. You'll arise, then and there, as your own higher Self.

65. FIRST JOY

With the transmission of grace from the Guru you no longer seek solely to fulfill your desires and needs. You develop a love for that aspect of God that can only be called the truth. Like an addict, you become sensitized to truth and seek it out. At the same time, the grace begins to neutralize the hungers, appetites, and desires within the psyche—all of which are transubstantiated into one taste called the truth.

This experience has been called the first joy— seeking and finding the one taste in all things, the flavor of truth itself. And rather than being caught on the surface of phenomena, your heart and mind go spontaneously to the deepest inner truth of a thing.

DIVINE FIRE

SHAKTIPAT

TRANSFORMATION

THE STRUGGLE

66. Transformation

The energy of shaktipat, when transmitted into your system, carries the signal of awakening. Only a single atom is required for each person. Shaktipat is a profound and secret message that carries the voice of the Self, the speech of God. It comes not out of heaven in a fiery chariot, but as a thief in the night. Silently inserted, it begins to transform you.

Once received, your life is never the same. From that day forward you will carry the light of awakening physically within you. You will nurture it and accumulate it. You'll cause it to grow until it overwhelms your consciousness, burning away confusion and forgetfulness like the sun burns away clouds.

67. The Struggle

Shaktipat cannot fail. It's not a matter of if you will awaken, but when you will. Awakening is regulated by the grace of God, your own skill, the intensity of your nature, and the pressure you are capable of enduring in the transformation process. The capacity to endure, like anything else, increases with exposure.

But what causes pressure eventually causes pain. Often you'll feel pain when the points of mutability within your system resist the light of truth. That is a conversation with God and it always goes one way: you bend to God's will. The only variant is time— how long you choose to struggle against God's will.

KUNDALINI

UDHANA

INTENSIFYING THE FIRE

RESERVOIRS OF KUNDALINI

ALIGNMENT

PRANA SHAKTI

WILDNESS AND COMMITMENT

DIRECT SPEECH

68. Udhana

When kundalini comes into contact with your internal circuitry, it produces a spiritual fire called udhana. This highest form of fire produces purification, empowerment, illumination, and awakening.

The only thing that limits your ability to consciously handle all the subtle tiers of awareness is your energy level. Therefore, live in such a way that you're gaining and storing spiritual energy. As that spiritual energy accumulates inside your being, the spiritual fire increases. When the sublime shakti comes into contact with your inner bodies, you will experience the ignition of udhana as a subtle spiritual pressure.

Live in such a way that the fire is always nurtured and increased. The benefits from this are improved physical and mental health, stability, equilibrium, power, and purification—it's all good.

69. Intensifying the Fire

First, recognize the connection of mind to the life force, and the life force and mind to the breath. Then, as an act of will, it's possible for every single breath to perform a yogic action of purification and intensification of spiritual fire. You do this by using the bellows breath. In the same way that a bellows impacts fire, this type of breathing acts on the kundalini. Every time you stoke your breath in this deep conscious way, the kundalini is amplified in the system.

It is the nature of life to be magnetic, and by using the bellows breath you draw more and more prana shakti into the time continuum of your mind and body. You draw greater and greater life force into your life dream, the dream that includes birth, growth, decay and death.

70. RESERVOIRS OF KUNDALINI

The kundalini exists within and pervades the entire human body. There are two profound reservoirs of this vital energy. One is at the crown of the head and the other at the base of the spine. The nature of the kundalini at the base of the spine is a coiled serpent, powerful, like the rumbling of an earthquake, like a blast of radiation. At the crown of the head, kundalini is like a deep lake, radiant and empty. The central nerve, the sushumna, is the pillar between the two reservoirs. As the vitality of kundalini flows back and forth between the crown of the head and the base of the spine with each breath, through its sheer magnetic force it begins to draw these energies into the stream.

You have to understand that kundalini is the substance of creation itself, and what you're doing by connecting it to the breath results in bringing the vitality of that awakening force directly on-line in your system. It will act upon you and change you. By increasing its charge in your system, it will illuminate and transform your nature.

71. ALIGNMENT

The kundalini is the force of creation. It exists in infinite formation beyond comprehension, but its most immediate face is a form of sublime and extremely subtle electricity that exists in the atmosphere itself. Kundalini exists in the fabric of time and space, between heaven and earth, and flows through reality like a force of nature.

The way to access the kundalini is by attuning the instrument of your being to this sublime and oceanic force of creation. You must find the language of alignment between the instrument that is yourself and this conscious force of creation, the divine shakti.

72. PRANA SHAKTI

The word spanda means pulsation. It's a throb of awareness, a vibration filled with consciousness. One extraordinary spanda is called prana shakti. The word prana means life or vitality and shakti means power. So prana shakti is the life force; it is the first face of kundalini, the creative energy.

Prana shakti is extraordinary. With the cycle of every breath, it makes the journey from the top to the bottom of being. It travels from the gross material physical body to the subtle physical energy body to the mental body to the supra-causal body and back again.

73. Wildness and Commitment

Because of the powerful energies involved with kundalini meditation, practicing it requires a similar commitment to that of jumping off a cliff and dropping a hundred feet to the water below. There's a kind of wild abandon to that feeling, a commitment of self in this decision. You need this commitment to get all of your circuits on-line because you use the instrument of yourself as the vehicle.

This is not an abstraction. Your body, mind, and being quite literally form a pillar between heaven and earth. As you feel the intense energies, you feel a great pressure. But the human form is an extremely powerful, high performance vehicle of consciousness. It can conduct oceans of the purest energy. It's all in knowing how. And like diving or anything else, there's only one way to learn: you have to do it.

74. DIRECT SPEECH

When you feel pressures surging and collecting in the heart or swelling in sushumna, or you feel light exploding in the brain and energies moving, that is the kundalini shakti talking to you personally. You need to listen to it. In the end, that's what meditation is about because enlightenment doesn't happen in one blinding flash—it's a sustained conversation from the depths of creation to creation itself.

ARCHITECTURE OF THE HUMAN FORM

THE HUMAN FORM

A RARE GIFT

FORM IS DESTINY

FINAL FORM

INVOLUTION

THE FOUR BODIES

SUBTLE BODY

SUSHUMNA

CLEARING OF OBSTACLES

75. A Rare Gift

Once you come into contact with a Guru capable of generating the seeds of shaktipat, great fortune has occurred in your life. Out of grace, out of the force of evolution, you have acquired a form complex enough to undergo the process of awakening—the human form. A human form is rare and difficult to acquire. Rarer still do conditions arise in any person's incarnation where there is the opportunity to awaken from a limited to universal identity. This gift is a grace from God.

76. Form is Destiny

In spiritual life, form is destiny. Any depth of understanding of that form leads you to believe that the entire destiny of a human being is to awaken. Every instrument of consciousness and awareness is designed to move attention in an extremely sophisticated way. In fact, one can go from the most mundane condition imaginable to the condition of universal consciousness in a single lifetime. The avenue, the pathway of that transition is found in the structure of the human form itself. Nothing need be added; it is simply a matter of understanding and realizing your own nature.

77. Final Form

The human form is said to be a final form. With the human form you have within your grasp everything you need to gain full realization and recognition of the supreme consciousness as well as gain equilibrium with the supreme unconsciousness. You have everything; you just need to put it all together. Nothing more need be added. It's a final form.

Now as a rule, once a person becomes a human being it's a steady march of increasing depth and sophistication of experience until you finally see that dawn of recognition in their eyes. Having exhausted the external search they begin to catch the idea of an internal search.

When a person is at that turning point, they come onto the screen of their Guru, the being that belongs to a long line of awakened souls starting from the original soul. Through the touch of the awakener, the perfect master, the process of involution begins. The main dynamic of involution is the recognition and experience of the fourth state. The master facilitates this process by the clearing of obstacles—helping you get out of your own way.

78. Involution

Evolution is the process of achieving a form complex enough to undergo the profound and radical transformation of consciousness. The process of involution is coming to understand the instrument you've finally acquired. The instrument I'm referring to is the difficult-to-acquire human body. Having acquired this human form, you have to spend an equal amount of time learning how to use it.

When you are born into a human form, you are born into an incredibly high-performance instrument, and, quite frankly, it takes awhile to figure out how to operate it. It's finally starting to work the way it's supposed to as you awaken.

The mind's destiny is to be extinguished and transformed. When you begin to move into samadhi and have the ability to switch off your mind at will, then you are getting a handle on operating the human form. That is the beginning of true existence.

79. The Four Bodies

The human form has four bodies of increasing subtlety: the physical body, which is the organizational point of matter; the subtle physical body, which is the organizational point of energy; the causal body, which is the organizational point of mind; and the supra-causal body, which is the organizational point of infinite consciousness. All four bodies are inside the frame of the physical body, subtle sheath within sheath within sheath.

80. SUBTLE BODY

When we talk about the progress of a sentient being, we are essentially referring to the development of the subtle body. Almost all the instrumentation of the human being is in the subtle body. The sushumna is in the subtle body. The chakras are in the subtle body. The channels and currents of prana, the nadis and bindus, the storing and elimination of karma, all reside in the subtle body.

81. SUSHUMNA

From the standpoint of the spirit, everything you are and everything you will be dwells in the sushumna. Sushumna is the fiber which runs from beneath the spine through the crown of the head and up into the space over the head. It is, in fact, the spiritual path. It is the illumination of the sushumna and its ultimate realization that is the essence of the path. It is the field that must be purified, ignited and awakened in the crucible of the spiritual fire. Thus, wherever you go you take your path with you. The Self arises within. Look within to find the truth. You need not look any other place.

82. Clearing of Obstacles

Most spiritual progress is seen in the development of the sushumna. How bright and full of light is it? How empty is it? Is it full of karma? Is the grace of the Guru present there? Is the kundalini moving within?

Clearing of Obstacles is a form of meditation that clears the sushumna of samskaric and karmic obstructions. These obstructions are aspects of consciousness that are the fruit of karma and are attached to the human form. Confusion and ignorance are the result of karmic obstructions along this pathway.

ATMAN

STATES OF CONSCIOUSNESS

THE FOURTH STATE

VEILING

POLARITY

AWARENESS OF THE 4TH STATE

FALSE TRUTH

ALL PERVADING

SAMADHI

83. STATES OF CONSCIOUSNESS

The first three states of consciousness—waking, sleep with dreams, and dreamless sleep—are relative to the four bodies. The waking state relates primarily to the physical body wherein the operations of the senses, the mind, and the prana are present.

However, as we enter the sleep-with-dreams state, the awareness of the body and the senses falls away. All we have left is the awareness of the mind and the prana. In this state, we operate inside a condition of pure thought that is culled from the memory of the mind.

Then as we shift into deep sleep, the physical body and the senses shut down and only the life force, the prana, is present. The mind is gone. The senses are gone. The body is gone. Spiritually speaking, this state of consciousness is one membrane away from Atman.

84. The Fourth State

When you awaken from the deep-sleep state, what's the first thing that happens? A sense of well-being floods the body. You say, "Oh, that was a great rest. I had a great sleep." And you think back, "What were my dreams?" You recall a point when you were dreaming and vaguely remember the dreams. Then there's this moment where you entered deep sleep and there was nothing. No dreams. The give-away—and I love this—is that you can remember being nothing. You can actually remember no body, no mind, no senses.

The sages tell us, "The mind, the body, and the senses make up the dynamics of the psychic apparatus. If the mind is gone, the senses are gone, and the body is gone, another center of consciousness must exist." And thus it is. The Atman—the fourth state.

85. VEILING

There is the ocean of infinite consciousness within us that is present as Atman, non-originated and self-born. Atman can never be tainted or stained or destroyed. It can, however, be veiled by the confusion of mind, much as the sun can be hidden by clouds. The conflict produced by the psychic apparatus lost in desire creates so many waves of agitation that one can't see through the fabric of mind to the underlying truth. From the standpoint of Atman, those beings incarnated inside the personal identity are unconscious.

86. POLARITY

Inside a human being we have two poles that are struggling for dominance. Awareness of the fourth state coalesces into a point of infinite consciousness called Atman, which illuminates the nature of every human being and is hard-wired into our system. The true I-consciousness arises from Atman in the fourth state.

The other pole is the ego reflex, the ahamkara. This, the I-making reflex of the ego, is a false ruler. Having staged a palace coup inside the castle of the psychic apparatus, the ego says, "I am the source of consciousness. I, the mind, am the source of all illumination." In actuality, this is a pretender that is not a source of light in itself, but is a reflection, more moon-like than sun-like.

The struggle of spiritual life is centered in the relationship of these two polarities of I. Sadhana is the process of moving the identity of the ahamkara, the I-making reflex of the individual self, and introducing it to the true I-ruler, the Atman, that is at the foundation of our own nature.

87. AWARENESS OF THE FOURTH STATE

The process of yoga is to make the fourth state conscious. Most people are not directly aware of the Atman, the fourth state, but that doesn't mean it doesn't exist. It just means that their true subjective identity is unconscious. It is veiled, but occupies the waking, dream, and deep sleep states. But it's doing so unconsciously.

Thus, people are constantly victimized by the dynamics of the five sheaths of maya. They are victimized because they haven't consciously recognized the fourth state where their true subjective I-consciousness arises. Once one has been introduced to the fourth state, the Atman, the process where consciousness becomes aware has begun. This is the essence of all spiritual work.

88. False Truth

The individual, operating unconsciously, has mistaken the non-Atman for Atman and is functioning as if this were true. If you accept the ego-based identity as the true Self, you are in error and must constantly substantiate that error. It's a false truth, and you have to serve that false god with action.

This is where the dynamic of desire comes into play. Serving the false god requires that you continuously feed the ego with offerings of desire to keep it solidly in place. If you don't, it will wobble and become insecure. When it's insecure it says, "I am unhappy," and that's when you experience your life as unhappy.

89. ALL PERVADING

It should be understood that Atman is That. In the form of Atman, a pure particle of the infinite consciousness is present within you. Atman is reality, and it carries no limitation as to cause or action. This means it doesn't have to remain in the fourth state, the fourth body, but actually flows into the substance and content of the waking state, the dream state, and the deep sleep state, thoroughly pervading them. Not only does Atman pervade these other states, but the vibrations of Atman are their very substance, their very content.

90. Samadhi

The word samadhi means intuitive knowledge of the highest state. There are a multitude of classifications of samadhi, but they can be broken down into two fundamental conditions: savikalpa and nirvikalpa.

Awareness of Atman, the universal consciousness, begins at the level of savikalpa samadhi. "Sa" means "with form" and "kalpa" means "thought construct." So savikalpa is the recognition of truth with form. In savikalpa samadhi you are aware of God but still have thought constructs. This is followed by nirvikalpa samadhi. "Nir" means "without." Nirvikalpa is the elimination of thought constructs, hence the elimination of the mind. Only the supra-mind is present. Once that shift occurs, there is a constant and increasing blast of Atman pervading all three states: waking, dreaming and dreamless sleep. You're awake but in the nirvikalpa state simultaneously.

There are many stages of attention within both of these states but what is taking place is the contact of the individual identity with the universal identity. The drop of water merges with the ocean. The totality of the ocean is in the drop, and the totality of the drop is in the ocean. Identity moves from a point of individual and separate identity to the utterly merged and commingled Self.

APPEARANCE OF THE WORLD

PERCEPTION

DÉJÀ VU

BENEFACTORS

EMPTINESS

91. PERCEPTION

Prana is the motivator of mind. It is the impulse—
the vibration—that moves through the fabric of
mind producing the experience of thought. Prana is
the dynamic behind all mannter of perception, the
ordering of the psyche, the architecture of identity.

Most people stay enthralled with the phantasmagoria
of appearance when this throb of prana flows from
the center of eternity into their sphere. The prana
animates and produces a wave inside the fabric of
your mind. You open your eyes and see the world.
You animate that world with qualities based on data
stored in memory from countless experiences.

92. Deja Vu

It's important to understand that the mind produces the fabric and dynamic of appearance and experience. This process occurs when the invisible nature of mind interacts with the intangible building blocks of the five elements. Your constantly arising experience of the present moment is produced by the vitality of the pranas mixing with the information of samskara, karma and the data of the memory base.

If you understand this process only on the surface, then all the important things will be happening at unconscious levels. Basically you will be watching a movie one lifetime after another, always forgetting the ending, always being surprised, even though it's essentially a repetition of the same film over and over again with subtle changes.

93. BENEFACTORS

As the veil lifts from your eyes, you see that reality is profoundly diverse and that spiritual opportunity comes to you through the grace of energies that can only be described as benefactors. Whether seen or unseen, visible or invisible, they are there. The day comes when you find yourself in a landscape populated with beings that have been waiting for you to snap out of it, to grow up a bit, and to awaken. It's a conversation that echoes down through the corridors of eternity—a conversation that has made shaktipat available.

94. EMPTINESS

If you are to thrive and establish mental and physical balance in the process of spiritual unfoldment, you must turn your attention from the permanence of things to the impermanence of things, from the solidity of things to the transience of things, from the existence of things to the emptiness of things. There is no separate existence.

Although reality seems to appear outside oneself, it actually appears inside the mirror of the mind. The objectification of appearance has been the mind's mistake in understanding its situation. The world's seeming permanence, even in its most sweeping expressions—the existence of the world, the existence of the universe—is utterly conditioned by and rests upon the principle of emptiness.

AWAKENING

TRANSMISSION

UNFAILING

MAGNETIZATION

BHAIRAVA

ILLUSION

UNFOLDMENT

95. UNFAILING

Once planted within your system, this ancient way of awakening people, this transmission of the vibration called shaktipat, is irresistible and unfailing. It only awaits the coming together of needed qualities — the grace of the Guru, the right conditions, and the ability and desire to undergo the process. Its most potent food is the hunger to know God.

96. Magnetization

At the moment of shaktipat, magnetization begins—purifying, opening, and awakening. Hunger to know the Self arises. The intensity of that hunger translates to what you are willing to pay, what you are willing to go through, and characterizes how fast unfoldment takes place. You experience a quality of surrender that in itself is a form of grace. It's something that unfolds in you as your spiritual awakening deepens.

97. BHAIRAVA

Bhairava is the capacity to reveal the supreme I-consciousness at any time, in any place, to anybody. It is a form of grace, and while it cannot be summoned or manipulated, it can be courted. The sages tell us that through righteous living and the de-conditioning of habitual thought, you can thin down the impact of maya and attract bhairava. Exalted personalities, sages, and Gurus—beings who are one with the truth—act as agencies of bhairava. Much the way a virus is transmitted from one person to another, by being in the company of such beings you can catch the effect of bhairava.

98. ILLUSION

There's no reason why realization need take more than an instant. When shaktipat occurs, you have in that very moment achieved complete and total realization. Only the mind, which is addicted to its pattern-like behavior, prefers to stay locked in illusion. The mind uses the power of time to produce the illusion that you are not awake. In reality, awakening happens totally, infinitely and completely in an instant. Once shaktipat occurs it's impossible to become more awakened.

99. UNFOLDMENT

Complete and total realization occurs at the moment of transmission of grace. However, since you live in a dream that believes in the dynamic of time and the fabric of the senses, you force your realization to unfold over time. This is important to understand, because most of you are going to have your spiritual practice spread over time. You're going to be doing this for the rest of your life.

Constant contact with the Guru is an invaluable tool in this regard. It smooths the rough edges, speeds things up, and boosts your energy. Seek the company of your teacher! The opportunity to spend sustained time with such a teacher is an extreme form of good karma and surprisingly rare.

THE PROCESS

AWAKENED FORM

ABANDON

RIPENING

THE GURU'S LINEAGE

ENLIGHTENED BLESSINGS

100. AWAKENED FORM

With the technology of yoga one can invent a form wherein the presence of God can commingle with the formation of being. This is considered an awakened form and a transformation. What was is now extinguished and gone, never to reappear. The qualities of the individual are dissolved.

101. Abandon

There's a point where grace and the dynamic of bliss come together in your consciousness to produce a psychological framework characterized as abandon. When you acquire abandon, you are in a condition where you will do anything, pay any price, to experience the Self. At that point, things begin to move very, very fast. You will be able to go through extremely intense spiritual processes, which at an earlier time would have been inconceivable. When it's time to do this, your life will take a form where it's easy to do. You'll be going through dramatic events with excitement, not thinking twice about doing it.

102. Ripening

The transmission of grace given by the Guru produces an instrument of awakening that is virtually perfect. All aspects of an individual are ripened, even those that lay deep beneath consciousness. At the same time, your identity is sustained, and your assembly of reality is preserved.

The main thing you feel is the pressure of the force of creation as the transmission moves through your system. Your life changes. Something was there and now it's gone. You feel yourself becoming clearer and clearer. How quickly you ripen depends on your hunger to know God. To what degree are you willing to surrender to this indescribable and unknown quality we call God?

103. THE GURU'S LINEAGE

You might think that being fully aware of all aspects of the process of awakening as it unfolds within you would speed things up. However, if you were aware of all the dynamics of grace as they moved through your system, you would immediately become disoriented and fearful. This would be deleterious to the process and end up slowing things down.

The Guru's grace is the ingredient that prevents this from happening. You don't want to enter the path without a Guru, and you want to look for a Guru that has had a Guru. This way you're not dealing with a single individual and his or her own personal level of realization. You're dealing with the cumulative effect of the transmission of grace as it has passed in an unbroken chain from Guru to Guru to Guru.

104. Enlightened Blessings

Blessings coming from the enlightened sphere carry the nature of enlightenment within them. These are called grace-waves. When you come into contact with such a blessing, you should draw it in and allow the DNA of that blessing to talk to you, to change you. The blessing will show you how to become the enlightened version of yourself. It will give you a glimpse of that Self.

TRANSFORMATION

UNIVERSAL IDENTITY

CULTIVATION

ABSORBING THE SELF

REALIZATION

105. Universal Identity

In the mystical states, it is possible to lose one's personal identity and take on the quality of universal identity. This occurs directly in the mystical states of samadhi. Savikalpa samadhi is the first step where one distinctly feels contact with the infinite ocean, the turiya consciousness. In nirvikalpa samadhi, the individual nature is immersed in universal consciousness. In this stage, the individual nature is extinguished as the flame of a candle is doused. It is no longer present, no longer seen. No cause emerges from that place, from that ripple, from that drop.

106. Cultivation

The infinite qualities of the Self are drawn into a singularity. As they become a singularity, the entire being begins to operate as a unit instead of in a divided fashion. When you're divided, one part of you does this and another part does that. This is the sign of an uncultivated human being.

The signs of cultivation reveal the amount of organization and unification present in your being. Cultivation is the first thing I look for in an individual. How much of this person is functioning consciously? That dividing line between the conscious and the unconscious is what spiritual training is about.

107. ABSORBING THE SELF

The impact of contact with the Self is cumulative. We soak it up like a sponge. The more we absorb, the greater the internal transformation. This is a basic principle of spiritual life. Thus, there is the admonition to come into contact with the innermost spirit again and again.

As an act of love and will, all the attention of one's being should be brought to bear on the ocean of the infinite Self. We should compress the space between the external appearance of reality and the true inner reality. Through that compression, we quicken the spiritual transformation. In the *Shiva Sutras* we are told that one should plunge into the Self again and again. This means on a daily basis.

108. REALIZATION

In the infinite timelessness before creation, God gave rise to the desire to know Itself. In that instant there was infinite creation, half supremely conscious and half supremely unconscious. As God's identity arose in infinite consciousness, the supreme subjective I-consciousness appeared. Then in the supreme objective identity, the God consciousness veiled Itself in the form of infinite multiplicity.

The tension between the unconscious and the conscious produced a dynamic through which consciousness now seeks to know itself. We could define that process as evolution, the lowest forms progressing through a series of higher and higher formations of consciousness unto the point where God reveals Itself to Itself, and God Realization, God Consciousness reappears.

All empty. It is as such.

GLOSSARY

Adamantine: Not capable of being swayed or distracted from course. Diamond-like hardness or luster.

Ahamkara: Aham (I) and kara (maker). Ego; the illusory identification with the world and sense of doership.

Atman: Divine Self, unchanging, immortal, beyond time and space.

Awakening: Realization of one's union with God.

Bardo: Bar (between) and do (marking point, island). Point between worlds; dream projection. Any established state of conditional being—life, death, rebirth, heaven, hell, etc.

Bellows Breath: Pranayama meditation breath technique.

Bhairava: Spontaneous rising of truth. The word is made up of bhai (projection), ra (maintenance), and va (withdrawal).

Bhukti: Worldly joy and fulfillment.

Bindu: Energy center the size of an atom. Point of

spiritual control of the consciousness at the level of mind and energy body.

Causal Body: Body of mental formations.

Chakra (lit. wheel): Any of the primary energy centers in the body suspended within sushumna. Psychic centers that illuminate and activate the brain. The primary chakras are Muladhara (root chakra), Svadhisthana (genital chakra), Manipura (navel chakra), Anahata (heart chakra), Vishudha (throat chakra), Ajna (forehead chakra), and Sahasrar (crown chakra).

Coiled Serpent: Kundalini at the base of the spine; sacrum.

Deep Lake: Kundalini at the crown of the head; interfaces with the Self.

Detachment: Concept that a person's karma is separate from the true Self.

Dharma: The Way. The study of truth.

Dispassion: The ability to absorb all qualities of existence into self.

Ecstatic Equilibrium: Supreme identity balanced with individual identity.

Enlightenment: Stabilization of God consciousness in the physical body.

Five Elements: The elemental basis of the universe: ether, air, fire, water, and earth.

Five Sheaths: The five coverings of an embodied soul that determine the personality and nature of individual consciousness. They are the body, mind, process of purification, intellect, and bliss.

Four Bodies: The four aspects of the human form: the physical (material) body, the subtle (energetic) body, the causal (mental) body and the super-causal body (Atman).

Grace: Gift from God.

Grace of the Guru: The means by which one can be liberated and circumvent the full process of the laws of karma.

Guru: The word Guru is comprised of gu (darkness), the formless hidden power of God, and ru (illumination), the beauty and luster of living beings. Teacher or Guide to spiritual illumination.

Ishvara: Foremost Ruler, Eternal Self, God. Supreme Ruler of the Universe. As much of God that can be known.

Karma: Law of cause and effect. Physical, verbal or mental action that shapes one's destiny.

Kundalini (lit. coiled one): Dormant spiritual energy held at the base of the spine and awakened by shaktipat initiation.

Liberation: Freedom from the cycle of birth and death. State of realization of oneness with the Absolute.

Lineage: The link of guru to guru to disciple and God; pathway of transmission of grace.

Mandala (lit. section): Sacred circle. Diagram to inner mystical states.

Maya: God's manifestation as the world; illusion.

Meditation: Any of a number of practices that focus, hone, or quiet the mind.

Mind: Matrix of ego, intellect, and conceptual formation. Psychic apparatus.

Mukti: Spiritual liberation.

Mundane Equilibrium: Individual identity.

Nadi: Pranic channel.

Nirvikalpa Samadhi: Nir (without) and vikalpa (form or conceptualization). The highest state of samadhi, beyond all thought, attribute and description.

Prana: Breath; vital energy; life force. There are five forms of prana: prana, the descending life force; apana, the ascending life force; samana, the mental and cyclical life force; viyana, the expansion and infusion of life force; and udhana, the compression of life force.

Prana Shakti: Vitality; power of the life force.

Pranayama: Breath control.

Sadhana: Spiritual practice; sincere spiritual endeavor; spiritual journey.

Savikalpa Samadhi: Sa (with) and vikalpa (form or conceptualization). Union with God; awareness of God while still having subtle identity and thought constructs.

Samadhi: Sama (intuitive knowledge) and dhi (the highest truth). Union with God. Bliss or absorption in God. Meditative supra-conscious state.

Samsara [Wheel of Samsara]: Objective world; the cycle of birth and death.

Samskara: Stored impressions of inborn desire. Action of the five senses.

The Self: Divine Consciousness; essential nature; supreme identity.

Shakti: Divine energy.

Shaktipat: Descent of grace that awakens the kundalini.

Shiva Sutras: A Sanskrit text, revealed by Shiva, consisting of 77 sutras. The major scriptural authority for the philosophical school of Kashmir Shaivism.

Spanda: Pulsation; throb of awareness; a vibration filled with consciousness.

States of Awareness: The four states of consciousness – waking, sleep with dreams, deep sleep and Atman.

Subtle Body: The energetic body of a human being.

Supra-causal Body: Innermost of the four bodies; Atman.

Surrender: Recognition and the eventual resolution of ahamkara; the absorption of individual will by divine will.

Sushumna: Primary nerve running from the base of the spine to the crown of the head. The possessor of all worlds, qualities and universes.

Sutra: Thought thread; verse.

Transformation: In a spiritual sense, liberation. The awakening process or shift from mundane to ecstatic equilibrium.

Transmigration: Passing at death from one body to another.

Turiya Consciousness: Ocean of consciousness; Supra-conscious meditative state.

Udhana: One of the five pranas characterized by pressure or cohesion; spiritual fire.

Unconsciousness: Field to be transformed and awakened.

Universal Identity: Paramatman; Supreme Consciousness.

Warrior [Spiritual Warrior]: Spiritual seeker with iron will and flaming heart.

Yoga: (lit. union): Path and method of unification

GLOSSARY

CPSIA information can be obtained at www.ICGtesting.com
Printed in the USA
LVOW131823080712

289147LV00001B/19/P